IRELAND

—Annascaul

BOVRIL PEMMICAN

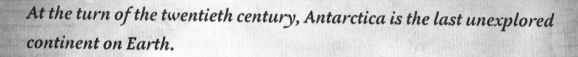

PROLOGUE

At the turn of the twentieth century, Antarctica is the last unexplored continent on Earth.

This time period is known as the Heroic Age of Antarctic Exploration. In England, the Royal Geographical Society, private investors, commercial companies, and the Royal Navy support expeditions to the southernmost place in the world.

The ice is unforgiving. It can break the human spirit. It takes many men willing to face hardship, danger, and years away from home doing jobs both big and small to keep these expeditions running. This is the story of one.

His name is Tom Crean.

N
W   E
S

THE INDESTRUCTIBLE TOM CREAN

· Heroic Explorer of the Antarctic ·

Jennifer Thermes

VIKING

TOM CREAN is born on the finger of a peninsula on a patchwork
island that points toward the wild and windy ocean.

But there is not much future for a poor lad from a large farm family
on the west coast of Ireland.

As so many of his countrymen have done for ages,
young Tom will take to the sea.

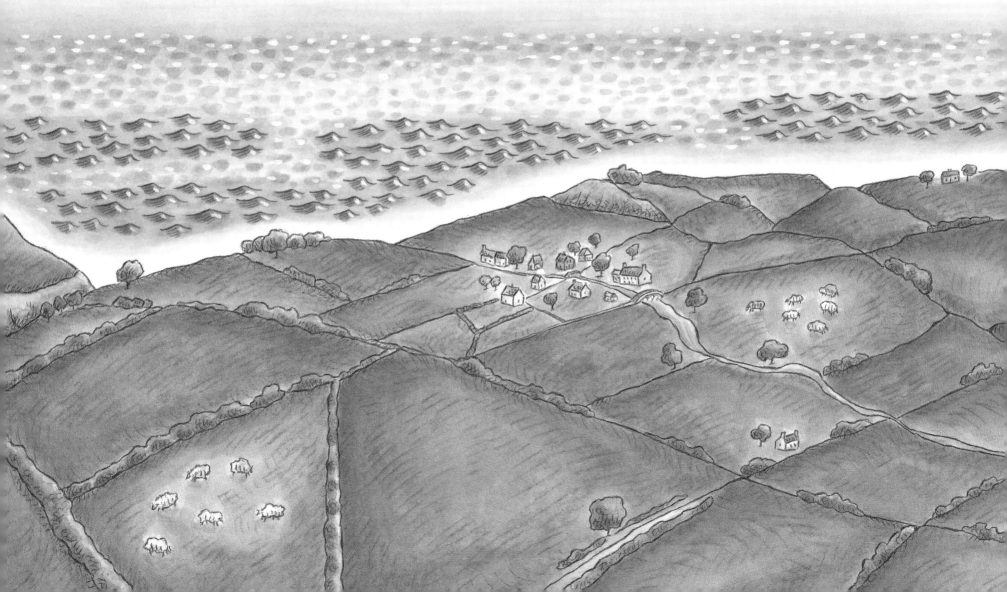

Tom joins the British Royal Navy. He is barely sixteen years old. He takes his knocks, and learns the ropes, and works his way up the ranks. He likely thinks often of home.

Ten years pass.

Ireland

England

EUROPE

ASIA

N

W   E

S

AFRICA

AUSTRALIA

New
Zealand

Tom is at port in New Zealand. The ship *Discovery* is ready
to leave for Antarctica—the frozen, uncharted end of the
earth! But a sailor has left the crew, and Captain Scott needs
a replacement, fast.

Tom steps up to the adventure.

ANTARCTICA

DISCOVERY

1901-1904

Robert Falcon Scott, CAPTAIN

Tom Crean, ABLE SEAMAN

Goal: to explore Antarctica and make scientific discoveries.

ANTARCTICA

South Pole

HUT POINT PENINSULA, McMurdo Sound

Tom and the men build a camp at Hut Point. For ten hours a day, they haul eight-hundred-pound sleds to lay supply depots on a route along the ice shelf, so that returning explorers can travel light and will have food and fuel on their way back to camp. The men know little of the ice's cold trickery. Tom learns quickly.

He sees the slushy floes that split and melt into the sea.

He warms the frozen feet of a crewmate, purple with frostbite.
He fears the hidden crevasses that plunge to a deep, dark end.

And yet, the ice . . .

. . . takes his breath away.

Winter comes quickly to Antarctica. The sea closes in. The *Discovery* is locked in the frozen McMurdo Sound.

The dark winter days and nights last from April through October. Explorations continue, but the ship stays trapped for two years. The Royal Navy sends rescue. It is a terrible thing to abandon a ship, but Captain Scott might have no choice.

Tom and the men chop channels through the thick blocks of ice and blast them with dynamite. Tom crashes twice through the surface to the bitter sea below. His mates pull him out, soaked to the bone and freezing. Tom is lucky.

Finally, the ice begins to thaw,
and the ship breaks free.
The *Discovery* sails for home.

Tom has earned a promotion for his good work.
In six years' time, Captain Scott will invite him
to Antarctica again.

TERRA NOVA

1910-1913

Robert Falcon Scott, CAPTAIN

Tom Crean, CHIEF PETTY OFFICER

Goal: to be the first to reach the South Pole.

GREAT ICE BARRIER (Ross Ice Shelf)

ROSS ISLAND Hut Point

South Pole

BEARDMORE GLACIER

POLAR PLATEAU

The *Terra Nova*'s deck teems with ponies, dogs, new motor-sleds for crossing the ice, and one rabbit that Tom has brought aboard the ship. But as they leave port, Captain Scott learns that Roald Amundsen, on the Norwegian ship *Fram*, is also trying to reach the South Pole. They must hurry.

A gale-force wind blows hard as they set sail. It sweeps one dog overboard and washes him back on deck again. Tom is surely relieved.

Tom and the men build a hut at Cape Evans to stay the winter. Once more, they make trips across the ice to prepare supplies for the long trek to the Pole.

Sometimes they use the dogs and ponies to pull the sleds. But the ponies are not fit for Antarctica, and Captain Scott is not used to handling sled dogs. The men must work even harder.

On one return trip—*CRACK!*—the ice splits beneath their tent. Tom and his crewmates jump from floe to floe and try not to slip into the sea. Killer whales circle and bump and knock against the bobbing ice. Hours pass. Finally, the men drift toward the ice shelf. Tom leaps across a span of water, scrambles up the slippery cliff, and runs for help.

The men are saved. But one sled and three of the ponies are gone.

For a short time after, Tom is snow-blind from the sun's bright reflection on the ice.

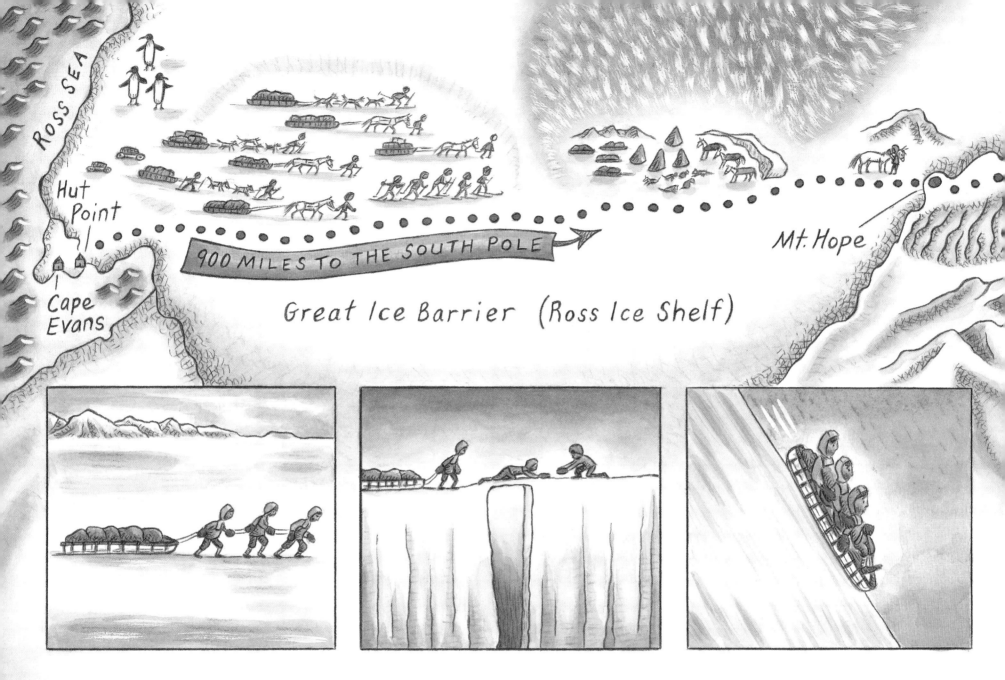

It is finally time to set out for the South Pole. The motor-sleds freeze and break down almost right away. The ponies lose their footing and sink deep in the snow. Teams of men and sled dogs are sent back to camp. A blizzard blasts across the endless white expanse, and the men are forced to stop and wait. They have been marching for ten weeks. Soon, there is not enough food for the animals. Tom must say goodbye to Bones, his favorite pony. And then, 150 miles from the South Pole, Captain Scott chooses four men for the last part of the journey. Tom is not among them.

Tom Crean, Bill Lashly, and Lieutenant Teddy Evans must return to base camp as fast as they can, before starvation and exhaustion overtake them. Evans gets sicker by the day with scurvy, which ravages a body in need of vitamin C. Tom and Lashly pull him on the sled. The men are tired. Evans begs to be left behind. Tom and Lashly refuse. Tom will go for help.

It is thirty-five miles across the ice shelf to the nearest hut. The cold bites Tom to his core.

He has only a few biscuits and a bar of chocolate to eat.

He must keep going.

Tom is completely . . .

. . . alone.

Snow swoops in behind him. Tom has found the hut just in time. Eighteen hours have passed. When the weather clears, Evans and Lashly will be brought back by dogsled. Tom Crean has saved their lives.

Later, Tom will smile and thank his long legs for carrying him across the ice shelf.

But for now, the men must wait the winter out at Cape Evans and hope that Captain Scott and the others will return from the Pole. They never come.

In spring, Tom and the search party find Captain Scott's tent. Scott and two of the men are frozen solid inside. His diary tells of their terrible ordeal. They had reached the South Pole after the Norwegians and perished on the return trip. The loss is almost too much for Tom to bear.

When he returns to England, Tom will be awarded the Albert Medal for his bravery. One year later, Captain Ernest Shackleton will ask Tom to join a new expedition. Tom Crean will return to the ice.

ENDURANCE

1914-1917

Ernest Shackleton, CAPTAIN

Tom Crean, SECOND OFFICER

Goal: to cross the entire continent of Antarctica.

South Georgia

Elephant Island

WEDDELL SEA

(ice pack)

RONNE ICE SHELF

It is August 1914. The *Endurance* departs with sixty-nine dogs, twenty-eight men, and one ship's cat on board. The whalers on South Georgia island warn Captain Shackleton that the ice is dangerously thick this year. Shackleton ignores them. Within weeks, they are trapped in the Weddell Sea.

Winter is coming. There is no radio. No one in the world knows where they are. Captain Shackleton says the pack ice will thaw, come spring.

The ice appears motionless. But currents deep below the crust swirl and push the *Endurance* far off course.

Tom and the men wait. They play soccer on the ice and hold Antarctic Derby races to exercise the dogs.

A surprise! Tom's dog, Sally, has four new pups! Tom names them Roger, Toby, Nell, and Nelson. He builds them a "dogloo" out of snow.

Winter comes again. Inside, the ship is cozy. The *Endurance* is stocked with tea, biscuits, and plenty of canned food. The men melt ice for fresh water and catch seals and penguins to eat, for a change. Tom mends gear and cares for the animals. The men read, write, play games, and even shave their heads one day for fun.

But the ship has drifted more than one thousand miles.
Ice wedges against its sides. The strong wood timbers
begin to pop and squeal.

The *Endurance* is being crushed.

They must abandon ship. Twenty-eight men move three lifeboats, tents, skis, food, and dogs to the ice. The ice shifts, and they move camp again. They watch as the ice slowly swallows the *Endurance*.

Land comes within view, but the men can barely drag the boats to reach it. They are floating north toward open sea. The ice is only six feet thick. Maybe they will never get off. They cannot care for the dogs any longer.

The ice can break your heart.

There is no time to lose. The men launch the three boats into the frigid water—the *James Caird*, the *Dudley Docker*, and the smallest, the *Stancomb Wills*—with Tom Crean at the helm. They aim toward Elephant Island. For seven long days, they sail, row, and slip carefully between icebergs.

The men set foot on a desolate beach. It is their first time on solid ground in over a year. But Elephant Island is far from any shipping lanes. No one will ever find them.

South Georgia
STROMNESS

There is only one choice. They must sail with the ocean currents across the most violent seas on Earth for help. The Stromness whaling station on South Georgia island is eight hundred miles away. Captain Shackleton chooses five crewmembers who are strong enough to make the trip. Tom Crean is one.

The *James Caird* is only twenty-three feet long. The men fit it with a stronger mast, canvas sails, and planking salvaged from the other two boats. They pack the hull tight with stones from the beach for ballast, to hold steady in the howling winds.

If they miss this tiny spot on the globe, they will be blown out to the vast Atlantic Ocean, and all twenty-eight men will be lost. They point toward South Georgia, and set sail.

Daylight. Moonlight. Stormy seas. Ocean swells. Seasickness. Soggy, spray-soaked clothes.
The men chip away at ice that freezes thick on deck and threatens to sink them.

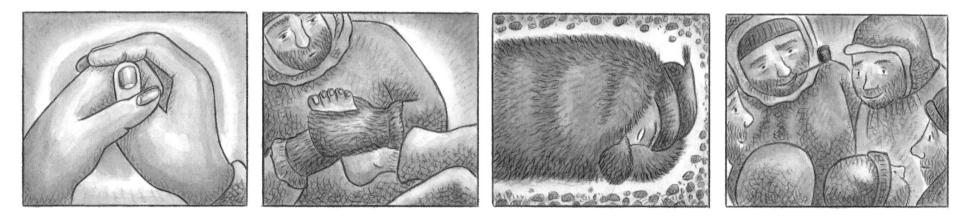

Frozen hands and frostbit feet. Salt water, sloshing. Rotting reindeer-skin sleeping bags.
Fitful sleep and hungry talk of lavish meals.

Tom balances a small stove fueled by seal blubber and cooks hot "hoosh" to drink quickly,
before it spills. They navigate by wit and pencil. They take turns at the tiller. They hope
their aim is true.

When it is Tom's turn to steer the tiny vessel, he sings quiet songs to himself. No one knows the words but Tom.

Suddenly . . .

The *James Caird* stays afloat. But their barrel of fresh water is now brackish with salt. The men become desperately thirsty. They have been at sea for more than two weeks.

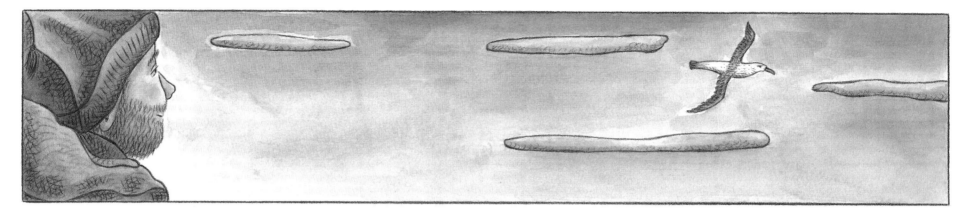

And then, a sign of land! But from nowhere, a storm races in and they are blown back to sea for another day and night.

Finally, closer . . . closer . . . and a surge of heavy surf carries them past jagged rocks, safely to shore. They have made it to South Georgia! The men find a cave for shelter and sleep.

In the night, wind and waves rip the *James Caird* from its mooring. Tom jumps in water up to his neck to save the boat, but the rudder has broken away. The whaling station is on the other side of the island. Knife-sharp mountains tower between the men and help. Now they cannot steer the boat, and it is too far to row.

Ernest Shackleton, Frank Worsley, and Tom Crean will cross the glacial range by foot.

It has never been done before.

Stromness
WHALING STATION

Peggoty
Camp
KING HAAKON BAY

Allardyce Range

SOUTH GEORGIA

The men set out by moonlight. They carry three days' worth of
food, a stove, and a carpenter's adze to use as an ice pick.

They nail screws from the *James Caird* into their soft leather boots
to grip the ice. They are linked together by rope.

The cold is relentless. The men stop only to drink a hot meal.
If they sleep for long, they will not wake.

They must keep going.

Climb up, race down.

One day passes. Night falls again.

They try to find the right direction.
(They do not have a map.)

The men must backtrack
one more time.

And then another.

Finally, they hear . . .

. . . the morning whistle at Stromness!

The three men are unrecognizable. They have not had a bath in months. But they have crossed the mountains of South Georgia in thirty-six hours. They have done the impossible!

The whalers at Stromness station send a ship for the men waiting on the other side of the island.

And four months and several tries later, the men on Elephant Island are finally rescued. Tom Crean and Captain Shackleton are in the boat that fetches them from shore.

All twenty-eight crewmembers of the *Endurance* have survived.

After the *Endurance*, Tom serves in the navy for several more years. He retires and returns to his beloved Irish home.

Tom never says a word about his Antarctic adventures. But his crewmates will remember the incredible, lifesaving feats he performed—fearlessly—during his time on the ice.

They will say that Tom Crean was as nearly indestructible as any man could be.

After the remaining men were rescued from Elephant Island, Tom Crean and the crew of the *Endurance* sailed to Chile, where their survival was greeted with great celebration. The men had been cut off from the outside world for more than two years. They came back to the turmoil of World War I. Tom and several others enlisted to fight in the war. Three of his crewmates lost their lives.

In 1920, Tom retired from the Royal Navy. He returned home to Annascaul, on the Dingle Peninsula, in County Kerry, Ireland. Sir Ernest Shackleton tried to convince Tom to join him on one more Antarctic expedition. Tom turned him down. (Shackleton perished of a heart attack on that final journey.) By then, Tom Crean had married a childhood friend, Ellen "Nell" Herlihy, and they had three daughters to care for. Tom and Nell opened a pub called the South Pole Inn—which still exists today!

At home, Tom was admired for his heroic deeds and adventures. But by all accounts, he never spoke of them. Ireland was fighting for its independence from Great Britain at that time. Because Tom had served in the English navy for most of his life, it is possible that he did not want to draw attention to himself.

Many of the officers, scientists, and private citizens who went on the Antarctic expeditions came from England's highly educated upper classes. They journaled, lectured, and wrote books about their adventures. Tom Crean did not. Yet he was noted in the writings of his crewmates as being loyal, courageous, and physically strong, and as having a raucous sense of humor. His mental endurance was especially admired during months of winter darkness, when he and his crewmates lived together in cramped ship spaces. And his ability to rally the men in the face of impossible odds of survival was a rare gift.

Tom's love of animals still shines through today in photographs of him caring for the ship's dogs and ponies. The animals met tragic fates. Though horses were considered the machines of their day, these ponies were not suited for the brutal ice and snow of Antarctica. And the British were not well trained in handling sled dogs, unlike the Norwegians, who had learned from the Inuit in the Arctic north. When circumstances turned grim, it was considered kinder to put the animals down rather than to let them suffer from cold and starvation. Those moments must have been among the hardest for Tom.

News of the death of Captain Scott and his team likely overshadowed Tom Crean's trek across the ice shelf to save the life of Lieutenant Teddy Evans. But Tom was awarded the Albert Medal for his bravery. Over the years, he went on to be recognized with three Polar Medals. Mount Crean in Victoria Land, Antarctica, and Crean Glacier on South Georgia were also named in his honor.

In the end, after the terrifying dangers and impossible conditions that Tom had faced on his own and as part of a team, an infection from a burst appendix did him in. Tom was sixty-one years old when he passed away. He had outlived many of his fellow adventurers.

An old sailor on South Georgia island reportedly warned Ernest Shackleton of the treacherous pack ice in the Weddell Sea with the words "What the ice gets, the ice keeps." Yet despite fearsome hazards, explorers were drawn to the Antarctic continent again and again. Surely, the ice had captured these men's hearts.

TIME LINE

1877—Tom Crean is born near Annascaul, County Kerry, Ireland.

1893—Tom joins the British Royal Navy.

1900—Tom is a crewmember of the ship HMS *Ringarooma* as it travels to Lyttleton, New Zealand. He joins the crew of the *Discovery* under the command of Captain Robert Falcon Scott.

1901—The *Discovery* sails for Antarctica and is trapped in the ice for two years.

1904—The *Discovery* returns to England.

1906–1908—Tom Crean works aboard several navy ships under Captain Scott.

1910—The *Terra Nova* departs for Antarctica.

1911—NOVEMBER 1—The trek to the South Pole begins.

1912—JANUARY 4—Crean, Evans, and Lashly start the return trip to Cape Evans.
FEBRUARY 18–19—Tom Crean walks alone across the ice shelf to Hut Point.
NOVEMBER 12—The search party finds Captain Scott in his tent.

1913—JANUARY 23—The *Terra Nova* leaves Antarctica and returns to England.
JULY 26—Tom Crean is presented with the Albert Medal by King George V.

1914—AUGUST 1—The *Endurance* departs England for South Georgia island.
DECEMBER 5—The *Endurance* leaves South Georgia to sail for Antarctica.

1915—JANUARY 19—The *Endurance* is trapped in the Weddell Sea pack ice.
OCTOBER 27—The crew abandons ship.
NOVEMBER 21—The *Endurance* sinks. The crew sets up camp on the ice shelf.

1916—APRIL 9–16—Twenty-eight crewmembers sail in three small lifeboats to Elephant Island.
APRIL 24–MAY 10—Tom Crean, Ernest Shackleton, and four other men sail eight hundred miles to South Georgia in the *James Caird*.
MAY 19–20—Tom Crean, Ernest Shackleton, and Frank Worsley cross South Georgia by foot.
MAY 23–AUGUST 30—The twenty-two remaining crewmembers are rescued from Elephant Island on the fourth attempt, with help from the Chilean ship *Yelcho*.
SEPTEMBER 3—The men arrive in Punta Arenas, Chile.
OCTOBER 8—The men return to Europe and World War I.

1920—Tom Crean retires from the Royal Navy and returns to Ireland.

1927—Tom and his wife, Ellen "Nell" Herlihy, open the South Pole Inn at Annascaul. They have three daughters.

1938—JULY 27—Tom Crean dies of an infection from a burst appendix at age sixty-one.

2022—The remains of the ship *Endurance* are found near where it sank in the Weddell Sea.

SELECT SOURCES

Alexander, Caroline. *The Endurance: Shackleton's Legendary Antarctic Expedition*. New York: Alfred A. Knopf, 1999.

Cherry-Garrard, Apsley. *The Worst Journey in the World*. New York: Penguin Books, 2005.

Discovering Antarctica. discoveringantarctica.org.uk.

Hooper, Meredith, and Bert Kitchen (illustrator). *Tom Crean's Rabbit: A True Story from Scott's Last Voyage*. London: Frances Lincoln Children's Books, 1999.

MacPhee, Ross. D. E. *Race to the End*. New York: American Museum of Natural History and Sterling Publishing Co., Inc., 2010.

Mason, Theodore K. *The South Pole Ponies*. New York: Dodd, Mead & Company, 1979.

Scott, Captain Robert F. *The Voyage of the Discovery, Volume I*. New York: Cooper Square Press, 2001.

Scott Polar Research Institute. spri.cam.ac.uk.

Smith, Michael. *An Unsung Hero: Tom Crean—Antarctic Survivor*. Cork: The Collins Press, 2009.

UK Antarctic Heritage Trust. ukaht.org.

Wilson, David M. *The Lost Photographs of Captain Scott*. New York: Little, Brown and Company, 2011.

Worsley, F. A. *Shackleton's Boat Journey*. New York: W. W. Norton and Company, Inc., 1977.

This one's for Tamar.
Slàinte!
-J.T.

VIKING

An imprint of Penguin Random House LLC, New York

First published in the United States of America by Viking,
an imprint of Penguin Random House LLC, 2023

Copyright © 2023 by Jennifer Thermes

Visit us online at penguinrandomhouse.com.

Library of Congress Cataloging-in-Publication Data is available.

Manufactured in China

ISBN 9780593117729

1 3 5 7 9 10 8 6 4 2

TOPL

Design by Kate Renner
Text set in Tactile ITC Std

The illustrations in this book were created with watercolor, colored pencil, and salt on Arches hot press paper.

The publisher does not have any control over and does not assume any responsibility for author or third-party websites or their content.

Orca (Killer Whale)

South Polar Skua

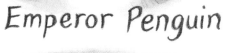

Emperor Penguin

Snow Petrel

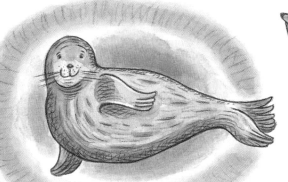

Weddell Seal

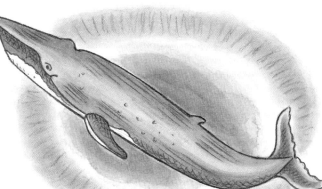

Blue Whale

Adélie Penguin

Wandering Albatross

Leopard Seal